THE DISAPPEARANCE OF THE UNIVERSE

THE DISAPPEARANCE OF THE UNIVERSE

ANDRAS M. NAGY

www.andrasnagy.org
ISBN: 978-1-963956-62-7

Contents

Foreword

Do you ever take the time to reflect on the nature of the sorrow that you experience within yourself? Have you ever pondered the reasons behind having a feeling of disconnection from the world, which in turn causes you to experience feelings of anxiety and desire?

Advaita is a strong way of identifying the core cause of suffering and ultimately putting an end to it. These questions are at the center of self-inquiry in Advaita, which involves asking oneself these questions. When it comes to Advaita, practicing self-inquiry does not include mindlessly embracing a set of dogmas or ideas.

Discovering the true nature of reality requires you to actively examine your own experiences and perceptions in order to fully understand it. Understanding the difference between the mental observer and the thinker is one example of this type of investigation. Through the process of perceiving the distinction between these two dimensions of awareness, we may start the process of dissolving the illusion of separation that is the source of so much pain in our current existence.

Obtaining freedom from the never-ending cycle of karma and transmigration is the ultimate objective of the practice of self-inquiry. In order to remove the layers of illusion that distort our view of the world, we can exclude the possibility of coarse items being candidates for ultimate reality and instead consider subtle objects to be candidates. Because of this process, we are able to look past the obstacles that lead us to feel fear and want. This process eliminates the sense of isolation that we have between ourselves and the world. The practice of Jnana Yoga, also known as the path of knowledge, offers a structure for introspection that is founded on the concept of non-duality. It inspires us to examine both the nature of our own existence and the assumptions and ideas that we have, and it motivates us to question those things. By participating in this sort of questioning, we may start to unravel the complex web of suffering that has trapped us for such a significant amount of time.

To summarize, self-inquiry is a potent instrument that may be utilized to gain awareness of the nature of pain that exists inside oneself and to put a stop to it. It is possible for us to liberate ourselves from the chains of fear and want that keep us bound to the cycle of suffering if we engage in non-dual inquiry with the intention of dissolving the sense of separation that exists between ourselves and the world. Let us then start on this voyage of self-discovery and emancipation without turning to any ideas or dogmas, but rather by simply questioning, investigating, and gaining an awareness of our own true nature

Duality

Have you ever stopped to think about the concept of duality and how it manifests in our lives? The illusion of duality is deeply ingrained in our perception of the world, but what if I told you that it is just that - an illusion?

Duality is the idea that there are two opposing forces at play in the universe - good and bad, right and wrong, light and dark. This way of thinking creates a sense of separation and conflict within ourselves and with others. But what if we were to shift our perspective and see beyond this illusion?

The truth is that duality is a construct of the mind, a product of our ego trying to make sense of the world. In reality, everything is interconnected and interdependent. We are all part of the same whole, and there is no separation between us and the world around us.

When we let go of the illusion of duality, we can find peace and harmony within ourselves. We can see that there is no need to label things as good or bad, right or wrong. Life is a continuous flow of experiences, and it is our attachment to these labels that causes suffering.

So how can we break free from this illusion? The key is to shift our focus from the external world to our internal world. By turning our attention inward, we can observe our thoughts and emotions without judgement. We can start to see that the true self is beyond duality, beyond the illusion of separateness.

When we let go of the illusion of duality, we can live in a state of oneness and unity with all beings. We can embrace the diversity of life and celebrate the interconnectedness of all things. The next time you find yourself caught up in the idea of duality, remember that it is just an illusion. Step back, take a deep breath, and remind yourself that we are all one.

Duality and suffering continue as long as the subject (con-

sciousness) is focused on any phenomenal object, whether physical or non-physical, and identifies with that object.

Dualistic Teachings of Spirituality

Much of current spiritual teaching focuses entirely on the waking world, thus becoming dualistic either by not understanding reality or by accepting a dualistic and anthropomorphic deity figure as God or Allah external to men.

Is this wrong? Of course, it is not wrong, but it can hinder one's spiritual liberation. Just see how religion can cause pain and suffering!

There are out-of-body methods, copious books written on karma and reincarnation that make some people think twice before acting out in bad faith, offering the dying hope that there is a new birth awaiting them.

Of course, there are benefits to yoga, meditation, and mindfulness. These practices, while beneficial, are dualistic models that will never lead to true liberation.

There are erroneous non-dual teachings mainly among neo-advaita when they claim;

1. "You are not the body, you are the Self"

Why it's dualistic: This implies a split between the body and the Self. While pedagogically useful, it sets up a duality between what you "are" and what you "are not," reinforcing separation.

True non-duality: In direct realization, there's no body or Self as separate entities—there's only what-is, undivided.

2. "You must dissolve the ego to realize the Self"
Why it's dualistic: It implies a process, a separate "you," and a goal ("Self") to be reached—clearly reinforcing subject-object duality.

True non-duality: The idea of an ego to be dissolved presupposes a self that has to do something. From a non-dual standpoint, no ego was ever real to begin with.

3. "Awakening happens to the individual and then there's abiding non-duality"
Why it's dualistic: The very idea of a timeline or stages ("first awakening, then integration") implies separation, process, and effort.

True non-duality: There's no one to awaken and nothing to integrate—this is it, as it is, now.

4. "You must meditate to realize your true nature"
Why it's dualistic: Suggests a separate doer (you) taking an action (meditating) to attain something (realization). This is the classic means-end structure of dualism.

True non-duality: Your true nature is always already the case; effort to realize it paradoxically conceals it.

5. "There is no self, only awareness"
Why it's dualistic: It sets up a new duality—awareness vs. self. "Awareness" becomes a subtle stand-in for a higher self or entity.

True non-duality: Even the distinction between awareness and phenomena collapses. There is no "awareness" of anything—just what-is.

6. "Everything is One"

Why it's dualistic: The idea of "oneness" often implies that there are many things that have become one—still a hidden multiplicity.

True non-duality: There are not many becoming one; there are not even "things." There's no subject or object to be unified.

7. "Consciousness is all there is"

Why it's dualistic: This reifies "consciousness" as a kind of ultimate substance and implies that phenomena are "within" it.

True non-duality: Even "consciousness" is too much—any concept implies division. True non-duality transcends both materialism and idealism.

8. "You are the witness"

Why it's dualistic: Sets up a subject (witness) and an object (witnessed). While it can be a useful stepping-stone, it's not non-duality.

True non-duality: Even witnessing collapses—there's no knower and known.

A Bit about Myself

Growing up, I always had a deep sense of curiosity about the meaning of life and what happens after we die. Coming from a religious background with a grandmother and mother who were traditional believers, I was exposed to the teachings of an antique illustrated Bible at a young age. While I was reading it, I found myself more drawn to the pictures than the text itself. I yearned for answers to my questions but found that religion only provided me with more questions and required blind faith in ancient texts.

As I entered adulthood, I veered away from religion and indulged in worldly pleasures such as chasing women and gambling. I lived a life filled with temporary satisfactions, but deep down, I still felt a void that needed to be filled. It wasn't until I reached my late forties that I met my yoga teacher who would change the course of my life.

Through a series of events, I stumbled upon an online video on Theosophy, which intrigued me enough to seek out further knowledge. This led me to my yoga teacher who offered a weekly program called Ancient Wisdom for the 21st Century. I found myself drawn to his teachings and eventually became his pupil.

Despite his insistence that he was not a guru, he opened my mind to new perspectives and practices that resonated with my soul. Through weekly meditation meetings and discussions on spiritual topics, I found a sense of peace and clarity that had been missing from my life for so long.

Meditating with my teacher was a life-changing experience that I will always cherish. His teachings were a unique blend of Eastern and Western traditions that provided me with a new perspective on life and spirituality.

Over the years, I attended his classes regularly and delved deep into the practices of meditation and the Ancient Wisdom.

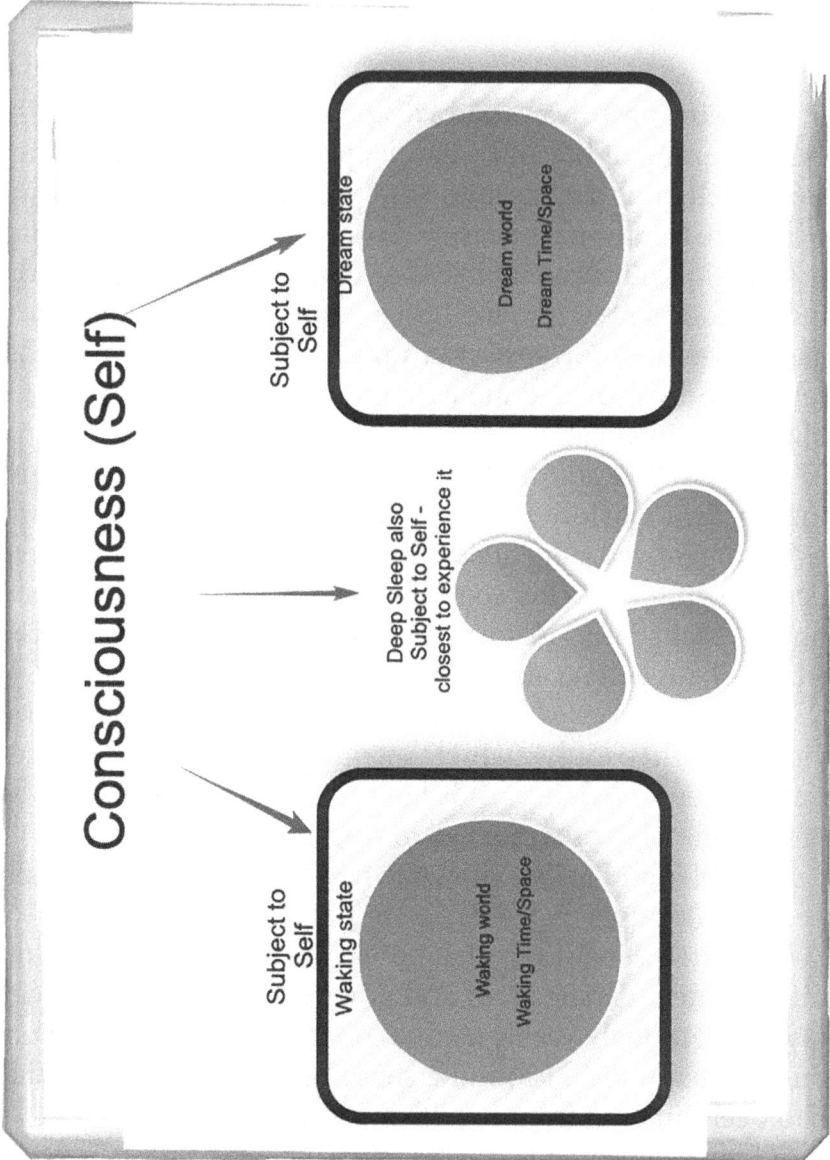

His teachings helped me confront my inner demons and fears, guiding me towards a path of self-discovery and inner peace.

When my teacher moved away to upstate New York, I felt a sense of loss and emptiness. I was still grappling with questions and doubts about the "Ancient Wisdom" that he had imparted to me. However, his teachings had left a lasting impact on me, and I continued my spiritual journey with renewed vigor.

I explored various spiritual traditions such as Kabbalah, Taoism, Tantra, and Mahayana Buddhism in search of answers to my existential questions. I delved into the teachings of Eckhart Tolle and The Course in Miracles, seeking further enlightenment and understanding.

My yoga teacher also introduced me to the concepts of reincarnation and karma, which intrigued me but also left me puzzled. How could I reconcile the idea of reincarnation with the timeless nature of existence? These questions lingered in my mind, urging me to seek further guidance and insight.

Meditating with my teacher had opened doors to a deeper understanding of myself and the world around me. His teachings had ignited a spark within me, guiding me toward a path of spiritual growth and transformation.

Though he may be physically far away, his presence continues to inspire me on my spiritual journey. I am eternally grateful for the time I spent meditating with my teacher, and I carry his teachings with me wherever I go, striving to live my life with mindfulness and compassion.

Today, I continue on my journey of self-discovery and spiritual growth, guided by the wisdom of my teacher and the ancient practices of yoga and meditation. While I may not have all the answers to life's biggest questions, I am grateful for the journey that has led me to where I am today. I have come to realize that the true meaning of life lies in the journey itself, and I am excited to see where it will take me next.

Waking State Bias: A Deeper Look into Consciousness

Have you ever stopped to consider how our waking state of consciousness might be limiting our understanding of reality?

In the field of Advaita Vedanta, a traditional Indian philosophy, the concept of "waking state bias" is explored to challenge the idea that our waking consciousness alone can provide us with a complete understanding of the world around us.

Advaita Vedanta suggests that human consciousness is not limited to just our waking state. In fact, it posits that there are three main states of consciousness: waking, dreaming, and deep sleep. While most philosophical and scientific systems focus solely on the waking state for knowledge and understanding, Advaita Vedanta takes a more holistic approach by giving equal importance to all three states.

By exploring consciousness through all three states, Advaita Vedanta offers a more comprehensive understanding of reality. It challenges the idea that the waking state is the only privileged state of consciousness and encourages individuals to look beyond their waking experiences to gain a deeper insight into the nature of existence.

This tri-basic method of inquiry into consciousness opens up new possibilities for understanding the world around us. It allows us to tap into our intuitive experiences and explore the nature of reality from a more holistic perspective. By acknowledging the importance of all three states of consciousness, we can begin to break free from the limitations of our waking state bias and expand our understanding of the world and ourselves.

In a world where waking consciousness is often prioritized, it is essential to consider the insights that can be gained from exploring consciousness through multiple states. Advaita Vedanta offers a unique approach to understanding reality that challenges conventional beliefs and encourages us to look beyond the waking state for a deeper understanding of the world around us.

So, the next time you find yourself caught in the trappings of waking state bias, consider exploring consciousness through the lens of Advaita Vedanta. Who knows what new insights and revelations you may uncover about the nature of reality and your place within it.

Since the dawn of time, numerous philosophical and spiritual traditions have devoted a significant amount of time and energy to investigating and debating the three states of consciousness: waking, dreaming, and deep sleep. Insights about the nature of the mind and our perception of reality can be gained through the experience of these states. While we are awake, we are completely aware of our surroundings and actively involved in the tasks that we do on a regular basis. An active mind is one that processes information and makes judgments depending on the stimuli that come from the outside world. The continual flow of ideas and feelings is a defining characteristic of this condition, which frequently results in feelings of tension and worry. On the other hand, while we are in a dreaming state, we transport ourselves into a world of symbolism and imagination.

Have you ever stopped to think about the relationship

between our dreams and our waking reality? They seem so connected to one another, yet there is a fascinating theory that suggests they actually cancel each other out.

The three states are nothing more than Consciousness manifesting in a state. But the observer of the state is not your waking ego! It is the consciousness that is the real Subject and all else is Objectified. Time and Space do not exist outside of the States, thus the States do not follow each other rather, cancel each other out, but that does not mean the canceled remains somewhere. It is gone, and then it reappears.

The dream world is in the dream state and the waking world is in the waking state, not the other way around! Time and space exists in the states, and objectified by consciousness.

Think about it for a moment. When we are dreaming, we are in a state where time and space do not exist in the same way as they do in our waking reality. Our consciousness is creating a new world, one that is completely separate from the physical world we inhabit during the day.

But then we wake up, and suddenly that dream world disappears. It is as if our waking reality cancels out the dream state, and we are left with only our memories of it. And the same is true when we fall asleep again - our dreams cancel out our waking reality until we wake up once more.

This theory suggests that the two states are not linear, where one follows the other in a predictable pattern. Instead, they coexist in a way that is constantly shifting and changing. One moment we are in our waking reality, the next we are in a dream world, and then back again.

It is a fascinating concept to consider, especially when we think about how much our dreams can impact our waking reality. They can influence our thoughts, emotions, and even our actions in ways we may not fully understand.

Despite the fact that dreams might be strange, incomprehensible, and irrational, they offer a glimpse into the conscious mind's subconscious. There is a possibility that we will encounter profound feelings, memories, and desires that are buried deep inside our minds when we are dreaming. The condition of deep sleep, on the other hand, is characterized by a profound sensation of tranquility and calm. The mind is free from ideas and other distractions when it is in this condition, which enables one to experience profound relaxation and renewal. A restful night's sleep is critical to both the physical and mental health of an individual because it enables the body to recuperate and rebuild itself. The cultivation of a mind that is clear and unadulterated is necessary if we want to comprehend the three states of awareness. We may cultivate the ability to examine our thoughts and feelings without becoming attached to them by engaging in spiritual activities like meditation and mindfulness.

Because of this consciousness, we are able to look past the illusions that the mind creates and become aware of our genuine nature. Eckhart Tolle, a spiritual teacher and author, views the mind as both a witness and the observed. Through the cultivation of a more profound comprehension of awareness, we can do this by acknowledging the existence of a universal self that is independent of both the ego and the physical body.

At the end of the day, the three states of consciousness provide a look into the intricacy of the human mind as well as the nature of reality. When we investigate these states with an open mind and a sense of curiosity, we have the opportunity to get significant insights about our actual nature and the fundamental nature of life. Philosophers, physicists, and mystics have long been fascinated by the intriguing concept of intuition. In many cases, it is characterized as a mode of knowing or understanding that does not include the use of logic or reasoning.

Some people have the belief that intuition is a more advanced sort of intelligence, as it may provide us with information and insights that go beyond what our conscious mind can comprehend. The ancient Indian tradition views intuition as a connection to the fundamental fabric of reality. There is a school of thought that holds that our real essence is pure awareness, which transcends the constraints of time, space, and individual identity. When one is in this condition, there is no distinction between the observer and the observed, nor is there any division between the self and the cosmos.

This more profound level of consciousness is accessible to us when we are in a state of intuition, allowing us to call upon it. A greater reality is accessible to us, and we are able to see beyond the illusions that the waking world presents to us. Along the same lines as the old story about the rope and the snake, we come to the realization that what we consider to be true may in reality be nothing more than an illusion. We are able to look beyond the veils of maya, which are the illusions of the material world, and catch a glimpse of the original nature of existence through the use of our intuition. Deep sleep is the stage in which we are most likely to experience a state of awareness that is unadulterated. This condition is characterized by the absence of any feeling of time or space, as well as any affiliation with the ego or the physical world. When we are in this condition, we are able to recharge and revitalize our mind, body, and soul. It is a state of complete happiness and regeneration. It's challenging to articulate or comprehend the concept of intuition.

A phenomena that defies logic and explanation is a phenomenon that is strange and elusive. We are all in possession of this talent, but only a select few are able to fully engage with it. Through the cultivation of our intuition through activities like meditation, mindfulness, and self-reflection, we can start to get access to a more advanced type of knowing and comprehension. In conclusion, intuition is a powerful and transformative force that can guide us towards a deeper understanding of ourselves and our surrounding environment. In addition to being a wellspring of knowledge and understanding, it is a gateway to more advanced states of awareness.

To be able to get this intuition. What's necessary for our minds? Which is normally extroverted and running from thing to thing; that mind has to become scattered from object to object. It has to turn away from the object towards the subject. Who is the subject of these objects? Who is the actual subject? So, the mind must become self-sufficient, introverted, and pure to answer that.

To be blunt, only some people are ready to intuit this way. That's called the spiritual faculty of the mind. We all have this faculty, but we must learn how to use it. We have an intellectual faculty. But that's of no use to you. We have these faculties, but that's of no use here. But the mind has an extraordinary faculty—its capacity to interfere and directly see that I'm not only the witness of my mind and my senses and thoughts but also the witness of the whole state.

To be able to intuit that, the mind has to become introverted. So suddenly, that faculty is called the spiritual faculty of the mind. Why? Because it's that type of mind. In that mind, can tune directly to this truth for itself.

Words can't describe this; only intuition can. The mind can't conceive of the witnessing consciousness, so it can't be known.

That mind can intuit the fact that I am the witness of the waking state. And I am not affected by anything that appears in the waking world. I am the witness to the dream. And I'm not affected by anything that appears in it. And I am the witness to their disappearance. We can intuit this truth here and now. Merely by examining.

With an introverted mind, whether the facts of the matter. Not how the waking mind looks at the dream and deep sleep. But what's the experience of the. That's the basis of this teaching. What is our experience? What does the world experience have to be understood to mean? What is our intuition about the three states? We don't experience them. We intuit them. So this is something to think about.

By developing our intuitive abilities and learning to trust the voice that comes from within, we can unlock the mysteries of the world and discover our life's true purpose. An Indian folktale described as "the snake and the rope." The wide and diverse collection of Indian folklore contains a story that has fascinated and perplexed entire generations. It is a narrative that penetrates deeply into the worlds of perception and reality, and it is the story of the snake and the rope.

Imagine a night that is completely black, and there is no moon. In the weak light, shadows move and forms change all around you. The environment might easily misinterpret a simple rope lying on the ground for something more dangerous, like a snake. An intense and tangible anxiety and uncertainty capture the mind when one sees what looks to be a deadly snake in the darkness. This fear and confusion are a result of the experience.

However, when daylight breaks and the truth is exposed, it becomes clear that the snake was nothing more than an illusion, a trick that the mind perpetrated on the individual. At one time, the rope was believed to be a snake; nevertheless, it is now understood to be innocuous and inactive, a harmless thing that has lost its scary appearance. Nevertheless, it is not the conclusion of the narrative. In light of the fact that the rope is swaying softly and the wind is blowing, it undergoes another transformation, this time becoming a garland.

The delicate petals and fragrant blossoms appear to arise out of thin air, therefore bringing forth a sense of beauty and peace that was not present before.

But where will the snake find its home? It was never a thing, which is a straightforward yet profound explanation. This scenario just involved the rope, which was a mundane and everyday object that was totally misunderstood for something else. The rope was the only thing that was genuine.

The story of the snake and the rope serves as a great metaphor for the illusions that can distort our view of reality. It serves as a reminder that despite appearances, things are not always what they seem to be, and that fear and confusion can distort our perception of the world around us. In a society that is rife with ambiguity and uncertainty, it is essential to keep in mind the lesson that the snake and the rope taught us. We are able to discover the truth that lies under the surface by questioning our assumptions and challenging our preconceived conceptions.

So when I dream, in the dream state, where is the waking state that was canceled? Is it in the background somewhere for me to wake up?

The waking state is like the snake when the light is on; it never existed in the first place until the light is off, and then it reappears.

This allows us to differentiate between reality and illusion and find clarity in the midst of uncertainty. When you find yourself in a situation where you are in the dark and confronted with anything that looks like a snake, it is important to keep in mind the story of the snake and the rope for guidance. See the world as it truly is, a place of beauty and wonder that dispels illusions and reveals the truth.

It is important to understand the mind's role in all this. The mind can heal and create miracles, and its potential is far beyond human understanding from a medical point of view.

The Experiencer: Understanding the Three States of Consciousness

Have you ever stopped to think about who is experiencing your reality in the three states of waking, dreaming, and deep sleep?

This is a deep philosophical question that has puzzled thinkers for centuries. But what if the answer is simpler than we think?

In the waking state, we make decisions based on our senses and logic. This is the reality in which our universe appears during our awake hours. We navigate our daily lives, interacting with the world around us and forming our sense of self. But who is the one behind the experiences in this state? Is it truly us, or is there something deeper at play?

Many spiritual perspectives and ideologies have tried to answer this question, but ultimately, it all comes back to the idea that the true reality is the one who is experiencing all three states. And that is none other than our Consciousness/Self.

When we dream, we are still experiencing reality in a different form. Our imagination runs wild, creating worlds and scenarios that seem just as real as our waking life. But at the core of it all, it is still us who is experiencing these dreams. The dream state is simply another aspect of our consciousness, a way for us to explore different aspects of ourselves and our desires.

Our ego, mind, and intellect, along with our ten sensory organs, turn outward in the waking state. The opposite is true when we dream in our sleep.

And then there is deep sleep, where we are in a state of unconsciousness. But even in this state, we are still the experiencer. It is a state of pure rest, where we are free from the distractions of the waking and dreaming worlds. It is a state of stillness and peace, where we can connect with our true selves without the interference of external stimuli.

So, who is the one experiencing all three states? It is us, the true self, the consciousness is behind it all. By understanding and embracing this concept, we can begin to see reality in a new light, one that transcends the boundaries of waking, dreaming, and deep sleep. We are the consciousness, and our waking reality is what we make of it.

You, your mind, and your senses do not exist outside of the state of waking. They arrive in a waking state. They occur in conjunction with the waking state. Now, this might not be easy to accept that my waking world appears only in my waking state in the same way - my dream world only exists in the dream state. When the dream ends, the dream world that appears in that state ceases to exist anywhere.

But in this waking world, we all have the natural conviction that this is the real world and it's not dependent on our waking state. *The fact is that no one has ever experienced the waking world independent of the waking state.*

As soon as the dream began, I identified with the dream body. I have dream senses, and I see the dream world. I consider the dream world to be real because I can see it, my dream friend can see it, and time and space are present. It all seems real at that time. Further, the contents of the waking world are equally canceled, the universe disappears to the ego/self[1]!

---

1   This is a nuance and many think the universe vanishes for everybody in the waking world. No so, YOUR Universe disappears until you wake up.

The difference between Thinker and Observer

In the world of Advaita, a profound difference exists between the thinker and the observer. While in our everyday lives, we often rely heavily on our thinking mind to navigate through various situations and make decisions, in the realm of spiritual seeking, it is the observer that takes precedence.

The thinker, in Advaita terms, is the conscious mind that is constantly churning out thoughts, analyzing, and interpreting the world around us. It is the part of our intellect that is conditioned by our beliefs, experiences, and societal norms. The thinker is essential for our day-to-day functioning, but when it comes to understanding the ultimate truth, it falls short.

On the other hand, the observer is the refined function of the intellect that has the power of discrimination or viveka. It is the part of us that can see beyond the limitations of our conditioned thinking and recognize the ultimate reality of Awareness. The observer is like a mirror that reflects the truth without distortion.

The shift from being identified with the thinker to awakening the observer can be challenging for many seekers. Our society places a high value on logical thinking and intellectual prowess, so it can be difficult to let go of the need to analyze and understand everything. However, in Advaita, it is not through thinking that we can realize the truth, but through direct experience and pure perception.

Advaita stands apart from other spiritual paths in its approach to the thinking function. While other paths may encourage controlling or quieting the mind, Advaita recognizes the futility of trying to stop the flow of thoughts. Instead, it teaches us to see through the thinker and recognize the ever-present observer that is beyond the realm of thoughts.

In conclusion, the difference between the thinker and the observer in Advaita is profound. While the thinker is necessary for our worldly existence, it is the observer that leads us to the ultimate truth. By cultivating the power of discrimination and learning to transcend our conditioned thinking, we can awaken to the reality of Awareness that lies beyond the realm of thoughts. In this journey of self-inquiry, it is the observer that guides us to the realization of our true nature.

Mandukya Upanishad – Verse 7

"na antaḥ-prajñam na bahiḥ-prajñam..."
"It is not inwardly cognitive, not outwardly cognitive, nor both. It is not a knowing entity like the thinker. It is ungraspable, beyond thought, unthinkable, the cessation of all phenomena — peace, bliss, non-dual — this is the Self."

Meaning: The Self (Observer) is not the thinker. It is that which is beyond thinking — the light in which thoughts appear and disappear.

Suffering and the Thinker-Doer-Experiencer

Impermanence and continual change characterize our reality. Whether it's the things we wear or the relationships we have, everything around us is certain to be transient. But, as humans, we have a propensity to attempt to direct and control these transient things in our lives. The source of misery is this delusion of command and control.

In the center of this anguish is the idea of the thinker-doer-experiencer. We consider ourselves to be unique beings who are always acting, thinking, and experiencing our environment. To the extent that we are oblivious to any alternate reality, this duality is intrinsic to our being.

It is easy to fall for the thinker-doer-experiencer fallacy and think that we have complete power over our lives and the world around us.

Frustration and disappointment are the inevitable results of an obsession with control. Everything we think, do, and experience becomes a part of us, and when that part of us changes or disappears, we feel a loss.

Recognizing the transience of all things is the key to breaking this vicious cycle of sorrow. Being able to release our attachment to the thinker-doer-experiencer requires an awareness of how fleeting and changeable everything is. Instead of resisting life's inevitable changes, we can accept them and learn to flow with them.

To escape the misery brought on by the thinker-doer-experi-encer, one must embrace the transience of all things and give up the illusion of control. Knowing that everything is happening just as it should and that change is an inevitable component of life allows us to be at peace and content in the here and now.

So, the next time you feel yourself mired in a never-ending loop of misery, step back and remember that everything is transient. Recognize that life is ever-changing and release the need to exert rigid control. When you do, you'll be able to accept and embrace the world as it is, flaws and all.

Gaudapada Karika 3.3

"Duhkham sukham ca sambandhāt utpadyete na kevalāt |
   sukhaduḥkhe hi nātmani sambadhau nāsti tattvataḥ ||"

"Pleasure and pain arise only due to relationship (with the body, mind, and objects), not from the Self alone. Since the Self has no real relation to anything, in truth, there is no pleasure or pain in It."

Insight: The Self (Ātman) is never the sufferer. Suffering only exists when identification with the thinker/doer/experiencer occurs. The Self, being free of all relations, is free of suffering.

The Emptiness of Awareness

Have you ever stopped to think about the nature of awareness?

It's easy to take for granted, but when we delve deeper into this concept, we realize that awareness is not as simple as it seems. In fact, it goes beyond being just a "substance", "thing", "attribute", "process" or "relation". It is something much more profound – a non-affirming conceptual designation for the nature of reality/ phenomena.

When we reach a point where the Witness collapses, bringing an end to all subject-object duality, we begin to grasp the true essence of awareness. It is not something that can be easily defined or confined to a specific definition. In the Vivartavada of Shankara, awareness is conceptualized as the "Eternal Subject" or the "Witness", standing in contrast to the ever-changing forms and objects of the world.

At its core, awareness is a non-dual knowledge that transcends the boundaries of time and space. It remains unchanged even after the Witness collapses, revealing its true nature beyond all causality. Shankara's teachings on Vivartavada were a stepping stone towards understanding awareness as existent, but he later retracted this concept in favor of Ajativada – a deeper understanding that goes beyond existence and non-existence.

This process of superimposing attributes onto awareness and then retracting them is a traditional method of teaching in Advaita, known as adhyaropa-apavada. It serves as a reminder that awareness is not something that can be easily grasped or confined within the limitations of language or perception.

In essence, the emptiness of awareness is a profound realization that opens up a whole new perspective on the nature of reality. It challenges us to go beyond our preconceived notions and dive into the depths of our own consciousness. So the next time you find yourself pondering the nature of awareness, remember that it is not just a simple concept – it is a gateway to a deeper understanding of the world around us.

Mandukya Upanishad – Verse 7

"na antaḥ-prajñam, na bahiḥ-prajñam, na ubhayataḥ-prajñam..."

"It is not that which is conscious of the inner (dream), nor of the outer (waking), nor both... It is unthinkable, ungraspable, featureless..."

This is describing Turiya — pure awareness. It is not an object, has no content, and cannot be described. It is empty of all phenomena — yet it is.

Object/Subject Relationship

It is important to understand the interaction between the two. When one delves into the area of object-subject connections, it is easy to become entangled in the intricate aspects of the concepts that are involved. Noumena, often known as the subject, represents reality in its existence independent of observation. On the other hand, the object, also known as the phenomena, is what we perceive through our sensorial experiences.

Consider a universe in which there is no awareness. For what reasons would the states be affected? It is now abundantly clear that the states are unable to materialize in the absence of consciousness. In a similar vein, think about the content of your ideas. To what extent do they possess the capacity to know themselves, or do they need to be conscious in order to see themselves? It is now abundantly evident that ideas, being things, require awareness for recognition. In essence, anything that goes through a process of transformation is considered to be an object or a phenomena.

It is impossible for these items to exist in their absence. The relationship between the subject and the object is unbreakable and inherent. Because of the dynamic relationship that exists between the subject and the object, our comprehension of reality is built on this basis. This occurrence highlights the interdependence between our perception and the surrounding environment. It is crucial that we realize the role that both the object and the subject play in creating our perception of the world that surrounds us as we navigate through the experiences that we have at this point in our lives. In conclusion, the link between the object and the subject is an essential component of both analytic philosophy and metaphysics.

This sharpens the deep relationship between our senses and the outside world. It is possible for us to get a more profound understanding of the complexity of life and awareness if we delve more into this topic.

My non-duality journey has led me to a profound realization: it is not against science. In fact, all the laws of physics, metaphysics, and evolution are true in the waking world. This may seem contradictory to some, especially those who believe that spirituality and science are at odds with each other.

However, I have come to understand that there is a harmony between the two. The waking-bias seekers may claim that if you are religious, you will never die. But the truth is, all the masters, gurus, and saints have died. Nobody has achieved immortality in the physical sense.

Death itself is natural, but how we die is an artificial construct created by society. Violence, aggression, and fear are all products of our conditioning and limited understanding.

When we die, what really happens? We only die in a waking state; just like when we die in a dream, it is not real. So why should dying in the waking world be any more real? Who is the one really experiencing death – the true essence of ourselves or the physical body we identify with?

It is a paradoxical truth that anything that can happen in the waking world does happen. Miracles are not impossible, but I choose to focus on self-examination and personal growth rather than getting caught up in the occult or supernatural.

My teacher once taught me about karma and reincarnation, concepts that are based on faith, speculation, and hearsay. While there may be individuals who claim to remember their past lives, I question the significance of this in the grand scheme of things for the real me – the eternal being that was never born and shall never die.

In conclusion, my non-duality is a harmonious blend of science and spirituality. I embrace the laws of physics, metaphysics, and evolution while also exploring the deeper truths of existence beyond the limitations of the physical world. Death is not real, as birth is a only true in the waking world. When you die in a dream you wake up, it is not real, similarly when your physical body dies it is not the real you!

Mandukya Upanishad – Verse 7

"na antaḥ-prajñam, na bahiḥ-prajñam, na ubhayataḥ-prajñam..."

"It is not that which is conscious of the inner (dream), nor of the outer (waking), nor both... It is unthinkable, ungraspable, featureless..."

This is describing Turiya — pure awareness. It is not an object, has no content, and cannot be described. It is empty of all phenomena — yet it is.

Drg-Dr̥śya Viveka (Traditional Vedantic Text)

"Rūpaṁ dr̥śyaṁ lochanam drik..."
"Forms are seen; the eye is the seer. The eye is seen; the mind is the seer. The mind is seen; the witness (sākṣī) is the true seer."

This is the clearest formal statement of subject-object discrimination in Vedantic thought.

Everything seen is an object.

The witness that sees all — but is never seen — is the subject.

Those who suffer from mental illnesses or depression, should keep in mind what Ashtavakra Gita says about this;

Depression is suffering. In the waking, dual world there are all kinds of suffering. Depression is just one of them. The goal of everyone should be to eliminate suffering by self-realization. Intellectually understanding what that is will not liberate you, but there is a poignant statement in the Ashtavakra Gita 1.2[2]

"If you consider yourself free, you are free. If you consider yourself bound, you are bound. As you think, so you become."

If the person is truly self-realized, he suffers no more.

---

2   I have published the Annotated Ashtavakra Gita - check it out on Amazon.

The Disappearance of the Universe: A Mind-Bending Perspective

The concept that the universe disappears might sound baffling and even absurd to some. After all, we live in a world filled with concrete objects, people, and events. How can something so tangible vanish into thin air? But what if I told you that the universe never truly existed in the first place?

For those who have delved into practices like meditation and studied philosophies such as Vedanta, non-duality, and Advaita, this idea may ring a bell. These teachings often challenge our conventional understanding of reality and invite us to ponder the nature of existence itself.

When we strip away the layers of illusion that cloak our perception, we may come to realize that the universe, with all its complexities and forms, is nothing but a fleeting mirage. In the grand scheme of things, the only enduring reality is the infinite, changeless consciousness that lies beyond the realm of objects and distinctions.

In this light, the teachings of revered figures like Jesus, Buddha, and Moses take on a new significance. While their words and deeds may have left a profound impact on humanity, they too were mere manifestations in the dreamlike tapestry of existence. As we awaken to our true nature as pure awareness, we transcend the limitations of the material world and see through the illusions that bind us.

In the realm of self-realization, the concerns and conflicts of the waking world lose their grip on us. The fluctuations of politics, global crises, and personal dramas no longer hold sway over our peace of mind. We become anchored in the unchanging presence of consciousness, untouched by the ebb and flow of worldly events.

It is a humbling realization that enlightenment, in its truest sense, eludes the grasp of the individual self. For to attain enlightenment would imply the existence of a separate entity seeking illumination, when in reality, all distinctions dissolve in the ocean of pure awareness.

So the next time you feel overwhelmed by the chaos and uncertainty of the world, take a step back and consider the possibility that the universe, as you know it, may not be as solid and enduring as it seems. Embrace the mystery of existence with an open mind, and perhaps you too will catch a fleeting glimpse of the disappearing universe.

In ultimate Self-realization both the observer and the observed disappear, because they are non-separate and mutually dependent, is a core realization in Advaita Vedanta, and the Māṇḍūkya Upaniṣad is one of the clearest expressions of this non-dual truth.

Māṇḍūkya Upaniṣad – Core Verse:

"It is not the inner (dreaming), nor the outer (waking), nor both (deep sleep). It is ungraspable, beyond empirical dealings, not inferable, not perceivable... non-dual (advaitam). This is the Self. This is to be known."

Key insight:

This verse points to the fourth state (Turiya) — pure consciousness — beyond subject and object, beyond all perception.

In Turiya, there is no division into observer and observed. Both collapse into the nondual Self.

Are you on a Quest to Find a Guru?

Seeking enlightenment through the guidance of a spiritual teacher? If so, you are not alone. Many people are on a journey of self-discovery, searching for someone who can help them navigate the complexities of life and find their true purpose.

But how do you find a true guru in a world filled with false prophets and charlatans? It can be a daunting task, to say the least. With so many self-proclaimed gurus out there, it can be hard to discern who is genuine and who is just out to make a quick buck.

One thing to keep in mind is that a real guru will never charge money for their teachings. They are not in it for financial gain, but rather to help those who seek their guidance. If someone is asking for exorbitant fees or promising quick fixes in exchange for money, they are most likely not a true guru.

Furthermore, a genuine guru will not seek to control you or manipulate you in any way. They will empower you to find your own path and make your own choices. A true guru will encourage you to think for yourself and question everything, rather than blindly following their teachings.

Another important aspect of finding a real guru is to look for someone who emphasizes experience over blind faith. A true guru will encourage you to explore your inner self and trust your own intuition, rather than relying on external sources for guidance. They will not claim to have all the answers, but will instead help you find the answers within yourself.

In conclusion, finding a real guru is not an easy task. It requires patience, discernment, and a willingness to look beyond the surface. By following these guidelines and trusting your own intuition, you can increase your chances of finding a true teacher who will guide you on your spiritual journey. Remember, the key to enlightenment lies within you.

Ah, the age-old quest for enlightenment. It seems like everyone is striving to reach some higher state of being, to evolve into the best version of themselves. But what if I told you that nobody actually gets enlightened? It may sound shocking at first, but bear with me.

The truth is, we were never born and we shall never die. We are eternal beings, simply experiencing this physical realm for a moment in time. So why do we feel the need to constantly evolve and improve ourselves? Perhaps it is the facade of individualism and ego that drives us to believe that we must always be striving for something more.

In reality, all we need to do is clear away this facade. Strip away the layers of ego and illusion that have built up over time, and we will find our true selves beneath it all. We don't need to evolve into something better, because we are already perfect just as we are.

Enlightenment is not some distant goal to be reached, but rather a state of being that is already within us. It is simply a matter of recognizing and embracing our true nature. So let go of the need to constantly improve and strive for more. Instead, focus on clearing away the distractions and illusions that cloud your true essence.

In the end, nobody gets enlightened because we are already enlightened. It is simply a matter of realizing this truth and living in alignment with our authentic selves. So let go of the need to evolve, and instead focus on clearing away the facade of individualism and ego. Only then will you truly find peace and contentment in this life.

When looking at learned Advaita teachers, you will see many who refer to their style as simply non-dualistic (or neo-Advaita). The pitfall of their teaching is that they claim, usually for membership, retreat fees, etc., that one does not need qualities to fully grasp the nature of non-dual existence.

Only attending satsangs is not enough. The quality of the mind turned inward is more helpful than any teacher or satsang. The tri-basic method is one helpful way to gradually achieve this quality of contemplative inward living. Patience and discrimination over time will result in an experience that one cannot explain. This is like being one with the universe and feeling intense peace and joy. No drug can rival this feeling, and many aspirants seek "enlightenment" for this temporal blip into infinity.

The purpose of life is to self-realize and stop the false idea of suffering. The one who suffers is a dream character. While at it, your dream character might help other dream characters to self-realize or at least begin to question the dream and seek the truth.

There is no need to get closer to anything, as everything is God and there is only God, except the name I use is Brahman. But you can call it anything that you are culturally conditioned to.

All else is a dream. Your consciousness is the same as the 8 billion dream characters's consciousness, and this witnessing consciousness will realize that all that is witnessed are dream characters (objectified); the subject, the consciousness, also gets dissolved, and only Brahman (God) remains. This consciousness (subject) with all the objects is a manifestation of Brahman, so the separation is just an illusion maintained by ignorance.

You are not the Thinker/Doer

Do you ever find yourself in a situation where you feel like you are stuck on a hamster wheel, unable to break free from the repetitive pattern of thoughts and actions? Okay, I'm sorry to be the one to break it to you, but you are not the one who thinks and acts. To put it another way, the fundamental core of who you believe you are is nothing more than a collection of thoughts bouncing around in your mind.

Everything you experience, including morality and immorality, likes and dislikes, seeking and becoming realized, and so on, is nothing more than the result of your mind continuously producing idea after idea. Some people find the idea of God to be reassuring, while others find it to be extremely burdensome. The concept of God is nothing more than a fabrication of the mind.

What is it that I am now writing? Yes, you may have predicted it; this is simply one more idea. It's mind-boggling to consider that everything we use as a foundation for our existence, from joy to grief, and every text that we adhere to is ultimately nothing more than a mental creation.

Therefore, what does this imply for you? Indeed, it suggests that the notions you hold do not constrain you. Your mind's limitations do not constrain you. You possess the ability to liberate yourself from the never-ending cycle of thinking and doing and to enter a new universe of possibilities and potentials.

Remember that you are not the one who is thinking and doing when you find yourself caught up in a tornado of ideas and actions the next time you find yourself in this situation. In comparison to the constraints of your thoughts, you are something far more vast and much more significant. Therefore, do not be afraid to liberate yourself from the constraints of your thoughts and fly into the boundless expanse of your authentic self.

Mandukya Upanishad – Verse 7

This verse describes the Turiya, the fourth state, which is beyond waking (jāgrat), dreaming (svapna), and deep sleep (suṣupti):

"na antaḥ-prajñam na bahiḥ-prajñam na ubhayataḥ-prajñam... sa ātmā sa vijñeyaḥ."

"It is not that which is conscious of the internal (subjective) world, nor that which is conscious of the external (objective) world, nor that which is conscious of both. It is not a mass of consciousness. It is neither simple consciousness nor unconsciousness. It is unseen, beyond empirical dealings, ungraspable, unassignable, unthinkable, indescribable. The essence of the Conscious Self alone is the negation of all phenomena. It is Peace, Bliss, and Non-duality. This is the Self that is to be realized."

Interpretation: The real Self is not the thinker or the doer — it is beyond all mental modifications. Thought and action belong to the waking/dreaming states (which are appearances); the Self is the witness.

Questions and Answers

Q: Since all souls will eventually reach Enlightenment, what happens when all souls reach Enlightenment?

I had a doubt that when all souls attain moksha what happens then, will the illusion still exist, I have this doubt because the method to understand turiya[3] is through this maya (according to mandukya upanishad). Does the turiya loses its consciousness again and enter the same cycle again?

A: In the ultimate reality, there are no souls! Everybody is currently enlightened. There is only the Self, also known as Parabrahman; nothing else exists. The concept of the soul is only applicable in the waking world, which is our known universe. Souls can evolve from matter and other stars in the expanding cosmos, but it's unclear from where they originate; they are simply the apparition of Parabrahman. Parabrahman presents the waking world to millions of "souls" without any restrictions.

Q: Why is awareness limited in dreams?

I am not talking about lucid dreams, but regular dreams, I'm completely aware and have zero control over my mind. What does Advaita say about dreams?

A: In the dream state of consciousness, the entire universe that was outside of us is now within us. Here, one is no longer aware of one's physical body. Each state has to be regarded as

---

3   In Hindu philosophy, turiya (Sanskrit: तुरीय, meaning "the fourth"), also referred to as chaturiya or chaturtha, is the true self (atman) beyond the three common states of consciousness (waking, dreaming, and dreamless deep sleep).

a whole manifestation of yourself. It's you that are appearing as the whole state. That's what a state is. A state is how you appear. It's not how you are because your nature never changes.

The subject-object duality is still there, but less dualistic. Subject and object are now in the same plane, like a mirror and its image. The subject has created the objects—in fact, the entire universe. The mind has created the universe. The dream state demonstrates that the mind compresses the time and space of the waking state, indicating that they are only objective realities. The dream state also demonstrates that the physical body is merely a mental projection, as it is completely absent in the dream state. Also, the physical body is not a real entity, as it does not exist in the dream state. The physical body exists in the , not the other way around. Finally, the dream state shows that the self-identity we hold on to in our waking state is also changing. For example, in my dreams, to date, I have dreamed of myself as a student in my school days. When I get up, paraphrasing Zhuangzi, the Taoist sage, I may ask, "Am I the man dreaming myself to be the school student, or am I the school student dreaming myself to be the man?"

Q: I believe in Advaita but I have some questions about karma.

They say that one that is born cannot be eternal. Unborn is eternal. Something unborn cannot die." Here is my question. If the cycle of rebirth was never started, meaning, there is no beginning or "first birth" it doesn't exist. So I can presume that I have had infinite births before, but the problem is, if there is no first birth, then, how can there be a last? If the cycle of rebirth never started, then how does it end after Moksha. How can beginningless have an end? Maybe I have misunderstood the concept of karma.

A: Upon Self-realization, the doer (kartā) identity dissolves. Since karma binds only the ego, the jñānī is no longer bound by sanchita or āgāmī karma. Only prārabdha karma (karma already begun) continues until the body drops.

As soon as you are self-realized, your karma will be burned up and you will be free!

1. Muṇḍaka Upanishad (2.2.8-9)

"When the seer sees the shining Purusha, the maker, the Lord, the source of Brahman, then having become wise, shaking off good and evil, stainless, he attains supreme unity."

"Just as a snake sheds its skin, even so the person discards the body and is freed from karma upon knowing the truth."

2. Bhagavad Gītā (Chapter 4, Verse 37)

"As the blazing fire turns firewood to ashes, O Arjuna, so does the fire of knowledge burn all karma to ashes."

Sanskrit:
jñānāgniḥ sarva-karmāṇi bhasmasāt kurute tathā

Q: Is deep sleep similar to be dead? Is death actually self realization as the ego is gone?

A: Not at all.

One has an experience in deep sleep akin to a dark wall. Consciousness remains aware of an empty mind devoid of vrttis (streams of streams consciousness.)
Less then this would be death, or the state between births.

Just like anesthesia or a drunken blackout happens instantly; no interval of unconsciousness is remembered. You wake up right away as the anesthetic needle goes in since the medications totally shut down even the mind free of any vrttis.

No, dying is not self-realization. To discuss a more subtle topic, "time" between births is eternal. Time is not even a concept since, while you're dead, none exists. Consider the times you dream in. When the dream started, can a dream person know? They reflect and find fake dream memories, a dream day, and dream occurrences that transpired. Since they are completely ignorant of the dream world, there is no way one could find when the dream began. Time is part of maya[4].

You will close your eyes when you die; it will be like opening them right away, sobbing as you leave the mother's womb. The intervals span an unmanifested universe. Your karana sharira(causal body) is the reason a physical body and mind seem to exist within space and time. Therefore, without body or mind, there is no space or time; only the possibility for the universe to show up via your karana sharira.

Q: Why do some spiritual teachers say we're already enlightened while others emphasize practice?

A: This is a good question; as practitioners of self-realization, we must walk a "razor's edge." There are irresponsible teachers who like shortcuts and always remind their followers, "You are already enlightened," and "There is no you" (ouch). The key is to delineate between the absolute and relative reality. Neo-Advaita, or, as they like to say, "non-dual" teachings, with some well-known teachers who make their living parroting the mantra of the absolute reality's facts while living in

---

4   The waking world's illusion

the dual waking world. It is like saying that there is no gravity in the ultimate reality; still, you should not try to fly or jump off a tall building.

The common sense approach is the traditional Vedic Advaita, which teaches certain preparations must be made in this dual realm (yoga, devotion, etc.). Of course, in the absolute sense, there is no death, birth, karma, or reincarnation, but those exist in the dream-waking world. You will surely die and very likely reincarnate until you reach a certain level of mind and spiritual maturity that would ready you for self-realization.

So this is the old conflict with neo-advaita and advaita/vedanta. One is ancient; the other is a bastardization of the ancient, tailored to the do-it-quick Western followers.

So the bottom line is you must practice to focus on the absolute daily, but you must realize that you still live in a dream-waking world and must act accordingly. Observe it, follow its rules, but do not identify with it. Try it; it works!

Bibliography

The Magic Jewel of Intuition: the Tri-Basic Method of Cognizing the Self by D.B. Gangolli.

Fuelless Fire: a Guide to Happiness by Anurag Jain

Special thanks to Ira Shepetin and his wonderful YouTube videos on this very subject.

Ira Schepetin (also known as Atma Chaitanya) studied in India under two important traditional teachers of Advaita Vedānta:

Swami Dayānanda Saraswatī (Dayānandaji) — one of the most respected modern Vedānta teachers, with whom Schepetin was the first Western disciple.

Swami Satchidanandendra Saraswati (Satchidanandendraji) — a renowned scholar-monk in the Advaita Vedānta tradition, with whom Schepetin was the only Western disciple .

These two deeply influenced his understanding and teaching of Non-Dual Vedānta.

www.ingramcontent.com/pod-product-compliance
Lightning Source LLC
Chambersburg PA
CBHW071742020426
42331CB00008B/2133